Harry The Whaler

George E. Sargent

HARRY THE WHALER.

By G. E. SARGENT,

AUTHOR OF

"HARRY THE SAILOR BOY," "STORY OF A CITY
ARAB," "RICHARD HUNNE, ETC."

LONDON:

THE RELIGIOUS TRACT SOCIETY.

56, PATERNOSTER ROW, 65, ST. PAUL'S CHURCHYARD,
AND 164, PICCADILLY.

HARRY AND THE BEAR.

[*Page* 89.

CHAPTER I.

HARRY CLARK was enjoying his holiday at his mother's cottage at Hazel-hurst*, when one day the postman brought him a letter. He soon broke the seal and opened the letter, which he found was from his uncle Gilbert; and then he read as follows:—

" MY DEAR NEPHEW,

" The Bible tells us, you know, not to boast ourselves of to-morrow, because we do not know what a day may bring forth; nor yet to lay plans for the future without thinking how uncertain they all are, so that we ought to say, ' If the Lord will, we shall do this, or that.'

* See " HARRY THE SAILOR BOY," published by the Religious Tract Society.

" Now, what do you think is coming after this ?
Nothing very dreadful or disappointing, I am
happy to say ; although it is something quite
unexpected.

" I have told you before now that a good part
of my life at sea has been spent in the whale
fishery ; and we have often talked together about
some of my adventures, and the sights I have
seen in among the ice-flocs and icebergs. Well.
instead of going out in the Industry again, I
have agreed to take another voyage to the
Northern Ocean in a whaler. It came about in
this way. First of all, our captain, Mr. Mason,
has made up his mind to retire from sea life
altogether ; and another is put in his place. I
have not much to say about this new captain,
only that from what I hear of him, he is not
one that I should very well like to sail under ;
and I am afraid that the Industry will in future
see a different sort of life, as regards morals and
religion, from what you witnessed on board.

" This is the reason I gave up my situation ;
and when I was looking out for another ship,
whom should I fall in with but an old shipmate
who is going out as master of a Greenland ship,
and who was looking out for a chief mate. It
did not take long to strike a bargain with him ;
and since then I have heard from the owners of

the Adventurer, which is the name of the ship ; and I am to go down to Hull, and be on board early in March.

" You may be sure, Harry, that I did not forget you in making these arrangements : and now you can have your choice. If you like to go out with me again, and your mother approves of it, there is a berth for you also in the Adventurer. But if you decide to part company with me, for any reason, I will get a berth for you in some other vessel as much like what the Industry was as I can : only you must write soon, and let me know your mind, that I may have time to look out.

" Why I put it to you in this way, Harry, is because there are some dangers in a whaling ship which there are not in another ; and I do not wish to persuade you to run into them. You know what these dangers are ; but I should like for you to talk to your mother about it, and tell her all that you have heard from me. As to common hardships, why, you are not the boy I have taken you to be, Harry, if you let the thought of them frighten you.

" As there is some time yet between now and March, I think I shall run down to Hazel-hurst to see your mother before taking this voyage ; but I shall not see you until you have made up your mind about these matters ; for I do not wish my words to weigh with you more than is right and proper.

"There is a good direction given to us all in the Bible, Harry ; and a precious promise added to it. The direction is, 'Trust in the Lord with all thine heart; and lean not unto thine own understanding. In all thy ways acknowledge him;' and the promise is, 'He shall direct thy paths.' If you go upon this tack, Harry, I reckon that, whatever you do, it will turn out to be the right thing at last."

There was a little more in the letter, which need not be put down here.

Harry Clark was not long in coming to a decision : after a few days he wrote to his uncle to thank him for his kindness, and to say that he would be ready to go out with him in the Adventurer.

After this, Gilbert Allen sent a parcel of books for his nephew to read. These were mostly accounts of different voyages that had been made in the cold regions of the north, and which Harry's uncle said would be both interesting and instructive. Harry read them with pleasure on the winter evenings which soon set in; and before he had finished studying them, his uncle himself paid the promised visit to Hazel-hurst.

"So, Harry, you have made up your mind to this voyage," said uncle Gilbert, as soon almost as they met.

"Yes, uncle."

"And your mother? what does your mother say about it?"

"It is all right, uncle: there isn't any hitch in that quarter."

"I am not sorry for that. I don't think I could have taken you out with me if there had been, Harry. I should not expect much good to come of it if you were to go against your mother's will. And you did not forget the direction and the promise I wrote to you about, I hope."

"No, uncle, I did not forget: I mean, I tried to do what the Bible says."

"And you think you are clear to go on with it, Harry?"

"I'll tell you all about it, uncle," said Harry, thoughtfully. "When your letter

came, I was so glad at the prospect of this
voyage that I should not have had any
hesitation about it if it had not been for
what you wrote: and then, when I did
turn it over in my mind more, I wondered
how I could know whether my going out
with you would be the right thing or not."

"Very natural, Harry: and what then?"

"Why then, uncle, I thought to myself,
I will pray for God's direction before I do
anything else; and then I'll put it to
mother. If she says, 'Go with your uncle,
I shall take it to mean that God approves
of my going; but if she says, 'Don't go,
Harry,' I must give it up."

"Ay, ay: you could not have done better,
Harry.   Well?"

"Well, I was afraid rather that it would
turn out contrary to my wishes: but I did
it, uncle. I prayed to God first of all; and
then I showed mother your letter, and told
her as much as I knew about the dangers
of that sort of navigation and of the
fishery."

"Quite right, Harry; and your mother
was not so much frightened as you thought

she would be: I am to understand that, I suppose."

"Mother was rather serious about it at first, uncle; and said she wished it was anywhere else that you were going: but then she said, too, that you had gone and come back a good many times in safety, and that there is the same Providence now as ever there was."

"Your mother is quite right there, Harry," said Gilbert Allen.

"And then she said that she would rather I should go with you where there is more danger, than without you where there might be less; and that as I had begun to be a sailor, she would trust me with God and you, uncle."

"And that made your way clear? Of course it did, though; and I am just so much of your mother's mind, Harry, that I would rather have you with me for another voyage or two, than that you should be cut adrift so soon. So there is nothing more to be said about it now, but to pray God to send us out and bring us back again in safety."

After this conversation, there was nothing more said about the dangers and hardships of a whaling voyage; but much was spoken about the stirring adventures which sailors in those seas fall in with; and Harry's uncle led him, as much as possible, to look forward to the new duties he would have to witness in others, or to perform himself. A few weeks rapidly and happily passed away; and, then, after affectionately bidding farewell to their friends and relatives at Hazel-hurst, Gilbert Allen and his nephew took their journey to London first, and thence to Hull by sea.

CHAPTER II.

HARRY'S LETTER. HE GOES ON BOARD THE ADVENTURER, AND HAS A CONVERSATION WITH HIS UNCLE ABOUT A CERTAIN CHART.

BEFORE we accompany Harry on his voyage, I may as well remind my young readers that whales, as well as multitudes of other living creatures, are useful to man. They are not, indeed, caught and killed for food, as many kinds of animals are; but the oil which is produced from their fat or blubber, and the substance called whalebone, are so valuable that every year ships go to the seas where whales are to be found for the purpose of obtaining constant and fresh supplies of these articles of common use.

I shall have to tell by and by about the capture of whales, and how they are dealt with when caught; but I may explain here that the fishing can only be carried on during the short summer of the polar regions; and that the ships and their crews which are

on this errand leave port in the spring of the
year, so as to arrive at these regions in proper
time to commence their work. There are
several ports in England and Scotland from
which whaling vessels take these fishing
voyages; and among these is the town of
Hull. "The Northern Whale Fishery," we
are told, "has in past generations been
looked upon with great favour" in this port.
At one time as many as sixty-three ships
sailed from it in one year. And at the time
of Harry Clark's boyhood, Hull was a busy
town in regard to this matter, as it is, in
some degree, even now; though the fishery
is no longer what it once was, principally
because there are not so many whales to
be caught as there used to be.

After this short explanation, I may go on
with Harry's history, and shall put some of
it in his own words as he wrote them in a
letter to his mother.

"MY DEAR MOTHER,
          "You will be glad to know that
uncle and I got safely to this port. We had a
rough passage from London, but I am happy to
say I was not at all ill; and uncle tells me that

I am no more like a landsman than I was when
I came off my other voyage. So I hope my
long holiday will not have done me much
harm.

"I have not seen much of Hull, only that
it seems to be a busy town; but I went
with uncle yesterday to the place where the
whale blubber is boiled down into oil. I cannot
say much for its being clean and sweet. You
know, when whales are killed out at sea, they
are cut up—I mean what is called the blubber
is cut up in great pieces, and stowed away in
the hold of the ship. Well, when the ships
come home this blubber is taken out and put
into very large coppers, and boiled till it comes
to oil. This is the most valuable part of the
whale; but there is whalebone too, which is
not the bone of the whale, as I used to think
it was, but a sort of sieve inside the mouth,
that serves instead of teeth. Uncle says that
its use is to catch the small fishes and sea-
insects which the whales feed upon, and strain
them off from the water. These bones grow
close together in the whale's upper jaw. There
are as many as six hundred of them in a full-
sized whale; and the length of the longest of
them is as much as fifteen feet. I do not quite
understand this yet, but I suppose I shall

when I see a whale ; and I hope I shall see a
good many before I get to Hazel-hurst again.

"I have been on board to-day for the first
time. The Adventurer is not quite ready for
sailing, but she will be in about a week ; and
before then I shall have to be at my duties.
She is a fine ship, three-masted, and rigged in
a different way from the bark I sailed in before.
There are more sailors too : uncle tells me
that when the crew is complete, there will be
nearly fifty in all. There are more men wanted
in these whaling vessels than in others of the
same size, because of the whale catching, which
takes a good many men away in boats at times :
there are more boats too ; but I cannot write
about these now. But I must tell you that
the Adventurer is double planked, to make her
stronger when she gets among the ice.

"I have not seen the master yet—this means
the captain, you know ; but uncle says he is
as good a sailor as ever walked a quarter-deck,
and a good man, as well ; so I think I shall
be comfortable, if I do what is wanted of me,
which I hope I shall.

"I do not know what wages I am to have ;
but uncle says I shall be as well paid as I
should be in any other service ; and besides
this, every body on board a whaler, from the

captain down to the boys, has a share in the profits of the voyage, according to the number of fish that are killed and the quantity of oil that is brought home. It is not much that will come to my share I reckon; but a little is better than nothing, mother.

"I do not remember that I have anything more to say now, only to send love to my sisters and brothers, and to tell you not to think too much about me when the wind is blowing at Hazel-hurst; for I hope I shall be kept in health and safety to see you again before next Christmas. Uncle sends his love too; and I am,

"Your affectionate son,
"HARRY CLARK."

A few days after Harry wrote this letter, he was taken on board the Adventurer by his uncle; but not before he was well fitted out with new warm clothing, which he was told he would be very glad of before long.

And now all was bustle on deck and below deck for some days, in making final preparations for the voyage: then the captain came on board; and then anchor

c

was weighed, and the Adventurer proceeded majestically down the Humber, and was soon out at sea with all her sails set to a fair wind, which, if it continued, promised a quick and agreeable outward bound voyage.

Harry's good conduct and character on the former voyage was of excellent service to him now; and he found that his uncle had kindly and generously procured for him a higher and better position than he had expected. Not that he had less work to do, however; for this, as Gilbert Allen knew, would have been no real kindness to him; but he had a berth in his uncle's cabin, and had opportunities of learning some of the higher branches of a sailor's profession, and of companionship also with the officers of the ship, with some of whom he messed (or had meals). Captain Smith, the master of the Adventurer, was also friendly towards him, in consequence partly of his relationship to the chief mate; but partly too on account of the good report he had received of Harry, and his evident activity and docility.

"I could not have done all this for you,

Harry," said uncle Gilbert to him when he explained to the grateful boy the advantages he was to enjoy, "if you had not behaved well on the other voyage."

"I am much obliged to you, though, uncle, for all that," said Harry.

"Well, Harry, we won't say anything about that. Near relations ought to help one another as much as they can, of course; and as it was altogether through me that you took up a sailor's life, I reckon myself bound to push you on as well as I can; but all I can do will be of no use, if you don't help yourself, as you have already done, Harry: you know that, my boy."

Yes, Harry knew that: he knew, or suspected at least, that it must be so in every calling; and that if a lad be not true to himself, it is not of much use for others to lay themselves out for his interests; and he was quite sure that it would be so on board ship. So, again thanking his uncle for all he had done, he expressed a hope of continuing to profit by his instructions and example.

"I have not much fear about that, Harry,"

said the chief mate, "so long as you don't neglect the chart."

"The chart, uncle?"

"Ay: you know, Harry, that no captain, in the present day, at any rate, would think of going to sea without charts, or maps, of all the seas, and coasts, and harbours, and so forth, he is likely to visit; with the soundings and dangerous places, rocks, currents, and all, plainly marked on them, as well as the different lighthouses on the coasts."

Yes, Harry knew that.

"And if he were so foolish as never to consult these charts, he would be likely enough to wreck his vessel, or get into some awkward scrape or other."

Yes, Harry could quite understand this too.

"Well then, Harry, the Bible is what I call the Christian sailor's chart on the voyage of life. It tells us our dangers and our means of safety; what course we ought to steer, and where we ought to give what may be called a wide berth. If we consult the Bible reverently, and go by what it tells us, praying earnestly for the Holy Spirit's help and guidance, we shall not, by God's bless-

ing, go wrong; but if we lay it aside, and
think we are wise enough to do without it—
what then, Harry?"

"Most likely we shall go wrong, uncle?"

"Sure to do it, Harry. There never was
a voyage in this world taken by any ship
that ever sailed, so full of rocks and quick-
sands, and perils of all sorts, as the voyage
of life. Thank God for giving us a chart, I
say; and let us take care to go by it. And
as to what some people say and would have
us believe, that too much Bible makes people
useless in common things of this life, I tell
you what I have seen all my life through,
Harry, and what I know must be. In the
first place, nobody can have too much Bible;
and, in the second place, the best men in
their calling, whatever that calling may be,
are those who are aided by God's good
Spirit in making the Bible their guide. So,
we won't give up the Bible, eh, Harry?"

It was not without good reason that
Gilbert Allen thus, from time to time, gave
this kind of advice, and impressed these
principles upon his nephew. He knew that
though the crew of the Adventurer was

composed of picked and steady men in
general, and though the captain and some of
the officers, as well as some of the common
sailors, were pious, God-fearing, Bible-loving
men, there were others who had no real
regard for religion, and who despised those
who had.   There was one officer especially,
Mr. Harris, the second mate, who, though a
good seaman, and a good-humoured, pleasant
companion (which made him more dangerous), made no secret at all of his scorn and
contempt, and his enmity against the Bible,
which he said was only fit for old women
and children ; though why it could be fit
for them, and not for such as himself, he did
not pretend to explain.

Now, Gilbert Allen knew how true it
is that " evil communications corrupt good
manners;" and he was anxious to strengthen
Harry's principles and to arm him against
ridicule.   It would have been a great grief
to him to see his nephew gradually giving
way to unholy influences, as it was a real
and increasing pleasure to him to witness, not
only his continued good conduct as a sailor
boy, but his thoughtfulness about eternity.

CHAPTER III.

SOME DESCRIPTION OF A WHALING SHIP. WHY ARE
WHALES SOUGHT AFTER?

As the weather continued fair and the wind favourable for several days, the Adventurer made capital progress, and, at the same time, the ordinary duties of all on board were comparatively light. Harry's uncle took this opportunity of giving his nephew some new and useful information respecting his future duties; and Harry examined with interest and curiosity the parts of the ship and her rigging which differed from those of an ordinary merchant vessel, as well as the formidable looking implements and weapons used in the whale fishery.

The Adventurer was a strongly built vessel, able to carry a burden of nearly four hundred tons. In the hold were stowed away a great number of empty barrels, and others which were at that time filled with water; and thus partly served as ballast, or weight, to keep the ship steady and sufficiently low in the sea. But these barrels were intended for another purpose; and Harry was given to understand that, should the fishing prove successful, they would return to port well filled with whale's blubber. Harry had already noticed, and written home to his mother, that the ship was double-planked; and it may be said here that all well built vessels, intended for whalers, are strengthened in this way: some, indeed, have three thicknesses of planks at the bow, and are otherwise "fortified," to make them more safe while sailing among the ice of the Frozen Ocean.

The boats of the Adventurer next attracted Harry's attention. They were seven in number, ranged three on each side of the ship, and one at the stern, so as to be ready for lowering into the sea at a minute's notice. "It would not do, Harry," said his uncle, "for us to be half an hour bungling about our boats when a whale is in sight. You may be sure it would not wait for us; and so we sling them in this way to be always ready."

They were good-sized boats, too, large
enough to accommodate five or six rowers
and a steersman, besides the harpooner, and
all his tackle; and built for great speed as
well as safety. We shall have to say something more about these whale-boats in
another chapter.

Mr. Allen also shewed his nephew the
implements used in whale catching. There
was the harpoon, a formidable weapon made
of iron, about three feet in length, with a
sharp pointed head, or mouth, as it is called,
which is thrown with such force at the
whales as to pierce into their flesh, and is
prevented from coming out again by the
head being barbed, like a fish-hook. Then
there were the fishing lines, made of very
strong rope, one end of which is fastened to
the harpoon; and these lines secure the
stricken whale until it is overcome. They
are of great length. Harry was informed by
his uncle that each boat carried with it between four and five thousand feet, or nearly
a mile of line; and as there were seven
boats to be supplied, there was of course a
large store of it on board the Adventurer.

Harry was then shown the lances used in despatching the whales after they were caught; these are iron spears, six feet in length, with sharp-pointed blades of hard steel; and he also saw the large knives and other instruments used in cutting up the whales when caught and killed.

"What are you thinking about, Harry?" his uncle wanted to know, one day during this examination, and when the uses of these various implements had been explained to him. What made Mr. Allen put this question to his nephew, was a look of thoughtful concern which he saw on Harry's countenance.

"I am afraid you will say that I am silly, if I tell you, uncle," said Harry.

"I fancy not, Harry. I think I can understand what you are thinking, without your telling me. You do not much like all these preparations for taking away the life of creatures that God has made : is that it?"

Harry confessed that it was : he could not make out exactly whether it were right to kill the poor whales and cut them up. "They don't do any harm, do they, uncle?" said he.

"No, they do no harm that I know of," said Gilbert Allen—"at least, they do no harm to us: perhaps the herrings and shrimps, and other small fish and insects which whales devour by thousands and tens of thousands, would think differently, if we could suppose them capable of thinking at all."

"But it is not because we take part with herrings and shrimps that whales are killed," returned Harry, with a little smile of triumph.

"No, indeed, that is quite true. You like a herring or a few shrimps, yourself, don't you, Harry?"

Harry confessed that he did.

"You have no objection to a good dinner of beef or mutton, or pork either, I fancy, Harry."

Harry acknowledged this also.

"But herrings and shrimps have life, Harry; and you could have neither beef, mutton, nor pork, if certain animals were not first killed; and these animals are all as much creatures that God has made as whales."

"I know that, uncle, of course."

"And you do not think it wrong to take away their lives, that you may feed upon them when dead?"

Harry had never thought of this before, and for a minute he was rather puzzled. At length he ventured to say that he did not think it was wrong.

"Well, I don't think it is wrong, either," replied his uncle; "but why then is it wrong to kill whales? They do not enjoy life more than sheep or bullocks, or herrings, I suppose, nor feel more in being killed. Is it because they are larger animals?"

No, of course that made no difference, Harry admitted: "but then, uncle," added he, "we don't kill whales for food, you know."

"No, indeed, that is quite true. Whales are caught and killed because we want oil. This is needed for a good many purposes, among others, for giving light in lamps. Before the way of obtaining gas from coal was discovered, oil was more necessary for this purpose than it is now. Can you tell me, Harry, what would be done for oil, if whales were not killed to furnish it?"

Harry might have replied that there are vegetable oils which could be obtained, though certainly not in sufficient quantities for all purposes for which oil is needed. He did not think of this, however, but rather hastily said —

"There are candles, uncle."

"And candles are mostly made of mutton fat; so, Harry, you would have more sheep killed that whales may be spared?"

Harry had not thought of this; and he could think of no more arguments just then in favour of the poor whales. "I said that you would think me foolish, uncle," he remarked.

"But I do not think you foolish. Your thoughts are quite natural: and indeed there are some excellent whalers who never see one of those huge animals overpowered and lifeless after a long ineffectual struggle, without feeling a kind of compassionate regret for the victim of their skill. But, on the other hand, Harry, it must be remembered that, from the very beginning, all living creatures in the world below man were provided by God for our use. You

may remember what is said in the first
chapter of Genesis : if not, get your Bible.
Harry, and look there."

Harry did so, and read as follows : " And
God said, Let us make man in our image.
after our likeness : and let them have
dominion over the fish of the sea, and over
the fowl of the air, and over the cattle, and
over all the earth, and over every creeping
thing that creepeth upon the earth."

" Well, Harry, there is not any doubt
in my mind that this gives us permission
to take the lives of birds, beasts, or fishes
—any sort of animal indeed—when wanted
for food or any other useful purpose. And
so it has been considered from the very
first. What do you say, Harry ? "

Harry thought of his beef and mutton,
and could not help assenting to his uncle's
views, especially as he remembered reading
in the Bible how God gave express permission to the Jews to kill some kinds of
animals for food; which would not have
been done if it had been against his laws.

" What we have to mind, Harry," continued Mr. Allen, " is that we do not

wantonly destroy life, and sport with the dying pains of any living thing. To kill anything just for the sake of showing our power, and without having any use for it when it is dead, I don't think is right. And to prolong or increase unnecessarily the sufferings of any creature which *will* be of use to us when dead, I am sure that is not right. But I don't see that this applies to whaling, Harry. We do want the dead whales; and I can tell you that no whaler ever wishes to make the battle longer than he can help."

Harry was pretty well convinced by his uncle's arguments: or, at any rate, his scruples were silenced; and he soon became as anxious as any one on board the Adventurer, to get on to whaling ground, as the seas frequented by whales are called.

CHAPTER IV.

THE Adventurer kept on her course
steadily, and after a few days' good
sailing reached the port of Lerwick,
in the largest of the Shetland isles.   Here,
Captain Smith and his crew employed
themselves in making final preparations
for the outward voyage, such as " *trimming*
the ship," as they said, and the completing
her ballast by filling with water such of the
casks as were yet empty.   The ship was
also divested of all elevated and gaudy
appendages to the masts and rigging, in
order that she might be better prepared
to meet the polar storms which were to
be expected.   The captain also laid in a
good stock of eggs, fish, fowl, and other
fresh meat; and completed his comple-
ment of hands   by engaging several
more seamen who were well used to the

whale fishery. This was such a busy time
that Harry had very little opportunity of
talking with his uncle, who, as well as
himself, had enough to do with his hands,
as well as with his head. There was
one proceeding, however, which excited the
young sailor's curiosity : and seeing his
uncle disengaged for a few minutes, he
asked what it meant.

"What are they doing at the top-gallant
mast-head, uncle?"

"Fixing the crow's nest, Harry."

Harry was no wiser now than before.
But he looked a little while longer before
he asked another question, and perceived
that the sailors were fixing a kind of
machine, as it appeared to him, on the very
top of the mast he had mentioned. This
machine was a framework of wooden laths,
not unlike a large barrel in shape, only
it did not bulge out in the middle : it had
an open top, and was covered all round
with stout canvas. In the bottom was a
trap door, or hatch ; and there was a
movable screen of canvas, which could be
shifted round the top of the machine, so as

to increase the height of it; and if Harry could have peeped into the inside, as well as observed the outside of this snug " crow's nest," he would have seen that it had a seat fixed to one side, and other contrivances for stowing away various articles.

"I don't know what a crow's nest is meant for," said Harry, presently, for he had never before heard the name as applied to any part of a ship's rigging, and had not happened to read of its use; and he was not ashamed to confess his ignorance.

"Why, you know, Harry, it is always necessary to keep a good look out, especially in seas which are encumbered with ice, to see when danger is coming on, as well as to have a good view of the sea all round, when it is open, to catch sight of any whales that may be about."

"Yes, to be sure, uncle: and I think I know now what the crow's nest is for," said the young sailor.

"Ay, I should not wonder," rejoined Mr. Allen. "You see, it would be neither very pleasant nor very safe either for any one to be at the mast-head, for hours

THE LOOK-OUT.

together perhaps, when the air is several
degrees below freezing point, and a brisk
wind blowing too, perhaps, enough to chill
all the blood in a man's veins."

"Of course it would not, uncle : but is
there always a look out kept from the
mast-head ? "

"Not always : but very often, especially
in dangerous situations, when somebody is
wanted there, with a good sharp eye, to
pilot the ship through packs of drift ice,
when everything may depend, under God's
good providence, on his skill. Sometimes
the master, or one of the officers, is obliged
to keep that station for hours together ;
and he might be frozen to death, in spite
of the warmest clothing he could wear,
if he had no shelter. But this simple
contrivance makes him snug and comfortable ; and the screen has only to be shifted
to any quarter the wind blows from, to
keep him completely sheltered."

The fixing of the crow's nest was almost
the last preparation to be made ; and the
Adventurer was then ready to set sail further north. It was now the beginning of

April; and Harry, who often thought of
Hazel-hurst and his mother's home, could
not help remembering, or rather imagining,
the cottage garden of his childhood, now
blooming with spring flowers, or fancying
himself for a moment in the glades of his
native woodlands and under the hedgerows,
gathering violets and primroses, and antici-
pating the bright warm English summer.
Even in the Shetland Islands, which are so
far north, spring buds and blossoms were
showing some tokens of life. But Harry
knew that he must give up all thoughts of
seeing spring or summer buds and blossoms
where he was going. He remembered how,
the Christmas before the last, he was scorched
with a midsummer sun in Australia; and
now, by way of contrast, the coming midsummer would, if all were well, be passed
amid ice and snow and storms. He did not
regard this, however, with any feelings of
dismay. It was all new to him; and he
was of that happy disposition of mind which
looks always on the bright side of circumstances. It is to be hoped, also, that he
remembered, with feelings of satisfaction,

that, wherever he might go, he would not be beyond the watchful eye and providence of his heavenly Father, whose promise to all who trust in him and love him, because reconciled to him by the death of his dear Son, is, that he will never leave them nor forsake them. And with such encouragement as this, he could cheerfully look up to God, and say, " Whither shall I go from thy Spirit? or whither shall I flee from thy presence? If I ascend up into heaven, thou art there; if I make my bed in hell, behold, thou art there. If I take the wings of the morning, and dwell in the uttermost parts of the sea; even there shall thy hand lead me, and thy right hand shall hold me."

There was one thing among others which gave great satisfaction to the young sailor, namely, that his present captain, like his former one, was not ashamed to acknowledge God in all his ways. I have said that many of the ship's crew were serious Christian men, for Captain Smith greatly preferred having such sailors when they could be obtained; but there were others who plainly did not fear God. Now, the pious captain

could not compel them to be Christians;
but he could and did make such rules and
regulations as kept the natural and evil
propensities of even the most careless and
hardened among them in check. He would
not permit profane swearing to be indulged
in; he took measures to prevent drunken-
ness, even when the ship was in port; and
he would have no more work done on the
Lord's day than was absolutely necessary
and therefore lawful and proper; while he
took care, whenever it was practicable, to
assemble the crew for Divine service and
public Christian worship. He commenced
this the first Sunday after sailing; and continued this godly practice to the close of
the voyage.

Some of the sailors sneered at this at
first; but before long they found the advantage, in so many ways, of sailing under
a Christian captain, that they left off sneer-
ing at his religion.

A week or two had passed away since the
voyagers left Shetland. During the first
part of this time, the Adventurer had been
favoured with a pleasant southerly breeze;

after this she had been some days becalmed, so that little progress was made; then came a head wind, and while beating about towards the north as well as they were able, the baffled sailors fell in with the first ice they had seen. It was *drift* ice, or ice broken up into large pieces; though there were only fragments of what had a little while before been probably a vast sheet, or field, so extensive as to cover a surface of hundreds of square miles.

Together with this drift ice, a great number of birds of different sorts were seen, so that though no land was visible, Harry judged that it could not be far distant. The birds were strange to Harry; and he was indebted to a friendly sailor for telling him their names, such as kittiwakes, boatswains, dovekies, and terns. He was also told that the Adventurer was at that time off the coast of Norway.

Having passed through the stream of drift ice, the Adventurer emerged once more into the open sea; and the wind changing again, the voyage was continued more rapidly.

" Well, Harry, what do you think of this now ? " asked his uncle one morning before they left their cabin together.

" I think it is rather cold, uncle," replied the young sailor, shivering, and with his teeth chattering so that he could scarcely speak.

A few hours before, Harry, who was in his uncle's watch, had paced the deck, and admired the bright gleaming lights in the sky after the sun had disappeared below the horizon, and enjoyed the calm, open, deep blue sea around, while he wondered how long it would be before they should get into what he called " cold latitudes."

" You did not know it was so cold when you turned in after the watch, did you, Harry ? " said Mr. Allen, putting on his pea-jacket.

" No, uncle," said Harry, following the good example set him : " but, uncle, what is the matter ? What have you been doing to your whiskers ? And only look here, uncle : why it is all snow, look ! " and he held up the blanket he had just left in his berth.

" Something like it, Harry ; but not snow,

either, exactly," said his uncle, laughing, and brushing from his cheeks the frozen breath which was gathering thickly on his whiskers in the form of hoar frost, as Harry's breath had also frozen as it settled on his blanket.

The scene on deck, when they reached it, was both strange and surprising to Harry, who compared it with what he had witnessed only a few hours before. The sailors were muffled up in thick warm clothing, which, however, did not seem to impart much comfort to them, for their cheeks were blanched and their lips were quivering as they hurried and shuffled to and fro. There had been a light fog, and a part of the rigging was encased in ice; so also was the deck, so much so as to make walking steadily upon it anything but easy, and to account for the shuffling gait of the sailors; so also were the sides and bow of the Adventurer, as Harry discovered when he looked over the bulwarks.

The cause of all this was very plain. The wind had suddenly shifted, and was now blowing a fierce, cold, cutting breeze from the north.

By the time the chief mate and Harry
reached deck, the fog had partly cleared
away; but it hung over the sea at a little
distance before the ship like a curtain. In
a few moments, however, this cloudy curtain
seemed to be rapidly lifted up; and at the
same moment, the hoarse voice of a man in
the rigging called out—

"Ice a-head !"

Every eye was now directed northward;
and then ensued a scene of bustle and
activity, without confusion however, while
the captain himself sprang into the rigging,
and ascended almost as high as the crow's
nest, and issued orders thence in a clear,
cheering voice, which were as cheerfully
and promptly obeyed.

Meanwhile, Harry, who had no particular
and urgent duties at that moment to divert
his attention, ran forward, and was filled
with surprise. The water all around was
agitated; and instead of the deep blue
colour it had exhibited a few hours before,
had become a dirty brown, while the sea
was no longer open. Stretching from east to
west, as far as the eye could reach, was a

"ICE AHEAD!"

vast quantity of ice, not more than a mile distant from the ship, and rapidly bearing down upon her.

Harry might have been a little alarmed at this novel sight if it had not been for the joyous expression on the countenance of an old experienced whaler by his side, as he cried out, "Ay, ay; this is something like: there will be something to do now."

"To get away from the ice, do you mean?" asked Harry.

"To get away from it! There's no occasion to try to get away from it, I reckon," replied the sailor. "No, no; we have got to get through it."

Harry did not at first see very well how this could be done; and as the ice kept swiftly bearing down upon the Adventurer, he could not help trembling a little in mind for the result. At the same time he heard the voice of the captain, who was now in the crow's nest, shouting with a clear, ringing voice, directions to the steersman at the wheel, while the chief mate was occupied in watching the vessel's course as she tacked about to take advantage of the breeze.

Harry, meanwhile, had nothing to do, and he stood still at the bow, forgetting, in his excitement, the uncomfortable feelings he had experienced from the sudden change in the temperature of the atmosphere. The old sailor seemed to have nothing to do, either, at that time, for he kept his station close by Harry.

CHAPTER V.

ARRY stood at the bow, watching the ice as it approached nearer and nearer, and observing the movements of the Adventurer, as, at one time she appeared ready to dash against the hard barrier which opposed her further progress; and then obedient to the helm and shifting sails, gracefully swung round, and slowly glided along the edge of the ice, and so near that Harry thought a biscuit might have been thrown on to it from the deck. It was several feet in thickness; and our sailor boy wondered what his present companion meant by saying they had to get through it. His wonder and surprise did not last long, however; for Harry soon perceived, what indeed could more easily be discerned from the rigging, that although the ice extended as far as the eye could reach in front and on either side

of the ship, it was not in one compact field,
but was broken up into innumerable pieces
with openings between them. Into one of
these openings the Adventurer was skilfully
piloted; and in a short time nothing was to
be seen around but large masses of thick
ice, so closely packed together in some
places that escape seemed impossible, but
offering openings elsewhere, through which
the ship slowly made her way, while from
the crow's nest above constantly sounded
the master's clear directions to the steersman and reefers.

Harry could not help, with some anxiety
asking the sailor at his elbow how long he
thought the Adventurer would be in getting
through the ice, and whether there was not
a little danger.

The old sailor smiled rather contemptu-
ously, but he answered civilly, that it was
uncertain how long a time it would take to
clear the *pack*; it might be a few hours, or
it might be a day or two; "and as to
danger," he added, "why, if you are afraid
of a little ice, you shouldn't have come out
here."

AMONG THE ICE.

"I did not say I was afraid," said Harry; "but whether I am afraid or not, there may be danger, you know."

"There's something in that," said the man; "and you don't look as if you would be easily scared. However, there is not much danger just now, I guess; though I have known danger come of being in among a pack of drift ice like this; ay, and seen it too."

"How was that?" Harry wanted to know.

"It was ten years ago," said the sailor: "I was aboard the Sea-Gull then; and if she had been a sea-gull in nature as well as in name, it would have been all the better."

"Why?"

"Why, because she wouldn't have been crushed to pieces then, as she was."

"But how did she get crushed to pieces?" asked Harry, who was naturally curious in such matters.

"Well, in this way it was. There's a good many sorts of ice, you know; leastways, it is called by different names, according to size and form."

Harry said he knew this, but his companion went on without noticing this. He had told the story of his and his fellow-shipmates' peril and escape very often, no doubt; and had always told it in one way, from which he did not choose to depart.

"Ay, there's a good many sorts of ice: there are icebergs, rising up out of the sea like mountains; hundreds of feet high, I have seen them again and again, with peaks rising up out of them sometimes, like church steeples. Very fine and grand they look, especially when the sun shines on them, when they come out in different colours like a rainbow. And high as they rise up above the sea, it is very well known there is more of them down below the waves than there is above; and that keeps them so steady.

"Then," continued the sailor, "there are what are called ice-fields. These are far north, and cover the sea so far that you might travel on them for days and days, for anything I know, and not come to the other side. Mighty thick they are too, ten or.

twenty feet, more or less, and covered with
snow as often as not.

"Then there are the ice-floes; these are
little bits of fields, perhaps a mile across
or so. After that comes drift-ice, like
this we are getting through now, where
it is broken up smaller than floes; and
when there is a lot of drift-ice together,
where no end of it is to be seen, as at this
present time, that's what we call a pack."

"And it was in a pack like this that the
Sea-Gull was knocked to pieces, was it?"

"It was, and it wasn't," continued the
old sailor: "it wasn't just an open pack,
where there's plenty of room to get in between; but it was pretty close up together
and all *hummocky*, piled up, you see, Harry,
one bit above another, and some of them
set up on edge, and then frozen together,
and standing up out of the water, as high
as a ship's bulwarks may be.

"Well, now about the Sea-Gull. She
was up in pretty high latitudes, and it was
towards the end of the season, so that it
was time to think of getting off home-
wards. But the fishing had not been very

good, and our captain was loth to go
back with only half a cargo; so we kept
tacking about from day to day, looking out
for whales that never came near us.

"All this time the ice was getting
thicker and thicker, and closer and closer,
till we began to think we should get
blocked up altogether; and at last the
word was given to make all sail southward.
That very day, a man at the mast-head
cried out that there was a whale, more
than a mile off, and in a few minutes all
the boats were in full chase. It was a good
while about; but the whale was caught
at last, and towed alongside the Sea-Gull,
while we set hard to work with the flenshing—that's getting off the blubbery parts,
you understand."

"Yes," said Harry, "I know."

"We were pretty eager about it, of
course," continued the sailor; "and we
did not notice that, while this was going
on, a storm was brewing; and if we had,
it would not have made much difference
mayhaps, for we could not have got out
of its way, though perhaps we might have

been better prepared for it. Anyway, on it came, such a gale as made us quickly furl all our sails, and then there was nothing else we could do but scud before the wind. The sea was uncommon rough, Harry; but that did not so much matter, or it would not have mattered if we had only had sea room. But that is just what we had not, for right ahead of us was a field of ice; and nothing less was to be expected than that we should be driven upon it and be dashed to pieces; for stout as the Sea-Gull was, we knew she couldn't stand such a shock. But, by God's mercy, when we were within half a mile of the ice, and expecting that in a few minutes more we should all be struggling for life without help or hope, the whole field, as far as we could see, began heaving with the fury of the waves; and then, it broke up with a noise like thunder, and in a few minutes the Sea-Gull was driven right in among the broken ice, without having even her bows grazed.

"I shall never forget that moment as long as I live," continued the sailor: "it

seemed as if our lives had been spared
almost by a miracle; and so indeed they
had. But if any of us thought that the
danger was over, and the ship was saved,
it was a mistake: it was not to be, Harry.
And very fearful it was to be tossing about
and driving on, with great masses of ice
all round us, dashing against each other
in wild fury, and splitting into thousands
of fragments as if it was to show us what
was to be our fate soon.

"Our captain was a brave man; and he
did all he could to save his ship and her
crew. He stationed himself at the wheel
with half a dozen of his stoutest men; and
what with his own skill, and with the
help of the men, he managed to hold the
vessel under some sort of control, and kept
clear of striking against the ice.

"After a while the wind fell; but what
was more dangerous than the wind, in our
circumstances, a thick fog came down
upon us before the sea had left off heaving
and swelling; and when we could not see
anything fifty yards before us, we could
hear the pieces of broken ice all round

running foul of each other, and breaking up with awful crashes almost every moment.

"At last our turn came, Harry. There was a shock that threw us all off our feet; and then another, and another; and there was not a man on board who did not think his last hour was come."

"What did you do then?" asked Harry.

"Do? what could we do but trust ourselves to the Almighty, and pray for his help? Not that we didn't try to help ourselves; but it was not much that could be done, for we had got jammed into the very thickest of the pack; and as far as we could make out all round us, there was no passage out of it. To make the matter worse, the ship had sprung a leak; and the sea was washing into the hold so fast, that twenty pumps could not have helped us; and when the mate and carpenter went below to see where the damage was, they found that the bow had been stove in so frightfully by the ice striking it, that the case was hopeless, and the only wonder was that the poor Sea-Gull kept afloat.

"But she did keep afloat just because

there was no room for her to founder. She
had got wedged in between two hummocky
masses of ice that held her up.

" It was hours and hours," continued the
old sailor, " that we remained in that
situation, and every hour made it more and
more desperate. The ice kept drifting on,
and our ship along with it; and at the same
time it was packing closer together. We
could feel it grinding the sides of the wreck,
and pressing them in: first one timber
giving way and then another, so that there
was no more chance for her than there is
for a nut in a pair of crackers. Our captain
saw this, and knew that the Sea-Gull was
done for.

" It was a great mercy that the boats
had not been injured: with all the knocking
about, the ice had not touched them; and
so there was just a hope that the crew
might be saved. So, as soon as the captain
gave the word, we all set to with a will.
First, the boats were lowered on to the
ice: then provisions and stores were got.
into them, with sails and warm clothing:
and when this was done, the captain called

all hands round him on the ice, for every
minute made it more and more dangerous
to be on the wreck.

" 'Now, lads,' said he, cheerily, 'we have
done all we can do, let us ask God Most
High to send us help out of his sanctuary ; '
and we all knelt down on the ice, while the
captain prayed heartily and earnestly for
deliverance, if it would please God to send
it ; or if he thought fit to take us out of
the world there and then, to prepare us
by his grace for the solemn change.

" We were a sad, thoughtless set, most
of us, Harry; but we were serious then :
and perhaps there were some prayers put
up at that time that God was pleased to
hear and answer too, for every man and
boy was saved, though the poor Sea-Gull
was lost."

" How saved ? " asked Harry.

" First of all, the fog cleared; and then
we saw plainly enough that the only chance
we had was to drag our boats over the ice,
which by this time was all jammed and
packed close together whichever way we
turned. As to the poor Sea-Gull, there

was no hope that she would ever float again."

"But," interposed Harry; "when you had dragged the boats over the ice, what could you do then?"

"Why, launch 'em to be sure, Harry," replied his companion.

"Yes, but you couldn't have got home in them, could you?"

"We did not expect it, Harry. But we might fall in with another ship, you see, for the whalers were not all returned; or we might get southward as far as Norway, may be, or Iceland. Anyway, it was not for us to give up, and settle down that we were to perish on the ice."

"Of course not," said Harry.

"Well, we did not give up," the old sailor went on; "and we did drag the boats over the ice. Hard work it was, for it was so rough and hummocky that we could not keep straight on, but had to go round about to keep clear of the worst parts; and, do what we could, we could not make more than a mile or two in a day. Then, though the ice was in general so closely packed

together, every now and then we came upon
a rift that we had to cross, and this hindered
a deal of precious time; so it is not to be
wondered that three days and two nights
passed away before we reached the open
sea.

"But we did reach it at last. There
were six boats, and eight of us to a boat,
besides the stores we had put in; so you
may guess we were crowded enough, to
say nothing of being a'most perished with
cold."

"But you were saved at last, you say,
all the ship's crew?" said the young sailor.

"Ay, ay, that's the main thing, Harry.
I was just coming to that. By God's good
providence, we had not been a day off the
ice, and were thinking sadly how many
chances there were against our ever reach-
ing England again, when a ship hove in
sight; and in six hours more we were
rescued. The ship was a whaler, of course,
and one of the last on the station; if we
had been a day later we should have missed
her, for she was on the point of sailing
home; and if we had missed her, most

F

likely we should never have been heard of from that day to this. As it was, we suffered dreadfully, some of us; but we all lived to get safe into harbour.

Harry listened attentively, though with a divided interest, to the old sailor's story. He had heard many such tales as these, and knew how true they were; but while thinking of these, he still continued to watch the progress of the Adventurer through the labyrinth of ice in which it was involved. Happily, no great danger was to be feared at this time, for the sea was calm and the wind became more favourable, so that in the course of a few hours the ship was clear of the ice.

Meanwhile, Harry remembered that he had business to attend to, more active if not so beguiling as that of listening to an old shipmate's yarn.

CHAPTER VI.

"THERE she blows. There she blows."

Harry was on deck when he heard this cry several times repeated from the crow's nest; and the next minute the Adventurer presented to his view a lively scene of activity and excitement. The men on watch who had, just before, been listlessly giving attendance to their duties on deck, and two or three of the officers who had been leaning over the bulwarks in quiet conversation, sprang to the ship's side, one of them overturning Harry in his eagerness, and commenced lowering first one and then a second boat on to the sea. It was so rapidly done, that almost as soon as Harry had recovered his feet, and while he was rather dolefully rubbing the elbow on which he had fallen, the two boats were lowered and manned, and in another minute they were being rowed swiftly away from the ship.

The excitement did not end here. From below men rattled up upon deck to take the place of those who had quitted the ship, and several leaped into and ran up the rigging to watch the progress of their companions. At the same time, the Adventurer, which was under easy sail, was put round a little to the wind, so as to keep more in the track of the boats.

Harry was among those who climbed the rigging; and as the day was clear and bright, he obtained from his station on the fore-top-yard a good view of what the hubbub was about.

The sea was almost clear of ice in the immediate vicinity of the ship; but a few large masses were drifting slowly towards the south at about half a mile's distance, and near to them Harry perceived a large black object floating on the surface of the water, and occasionally casting up what looked like jets of steam. It needed no conjurer to tell the young sailor that this large black object was a whale; and though

he felt some compassion towards it, in thinking of its probable fate, he soon became
interested in the chase which had begun.

In the foremost boat was Harry's uncle,
pulling the bow oar, for he was a skilful
harpooner; and, as chief mate, he was to
have the honour of striking the first whale.
Stowed in each boat were, among other implements, two harpoons with their lines; six
or eight lances; a small flag fastened to
a staff, to be displayed when the whale was
harpooned; an axe for cutting the line, if
necessary; a small bucket for bailing water
out of the boat, or for wetting the line, to
prevent the consequences of friction; and
in the first boat was also a winch for heaving the line into the boat again after the
fish was killed. All these things Harry
knew were required in the fishing, and were
always kept in the boats, ready for instant
service.

Very cautiously, though as swiftly as
possible, the boats were rowed towards the
whale; and as Harry was aware that these
animals, though dull of hearing, are very
quick-sighted, he was not surprised that the

rowers made a considerable circuit to get
behind that of which they were in chase.
It seemed for a little time as though they
had succeeded in avoiding the whale's sharp
eye, for it remained almost motionless on
the surface of the sea until the first boat
was very near; and Harry, who still kept
watching, could see his uncle ship his oar,
and taking a harpoon in his hand, rise on
to his feet. At that moment there was a
splash and a commotion; the enormous tail
of the whale rose high in the air, and then
the great animal had disappeared.

"Hurrah! well done, whale!" shouted
Harry, in the first burst of excitement, and
feeling almost ready, for the moment, to take
the poor creature's part against its hunters.

"Why, you young monkey, don't you
want the whale to be caught?" said some
one very near to him; and on looking round
Harry saw Mr. Harris, the second mate, at
his elbow, with a good-humoured smile on
his countenance.

"Yes, sir, of course; but—"

"But you want her to have a fair chance,
eh?"

CHASING THE WHALE.

Yes, Harry thought that was it.

"Well, she has got it now. By the by, what are you doing up here?"

"Only looking out, sir," said Harry, who was conscious that he had no particular business on the fore-top-yard just then.

"Idling, eh? That won't do, you know."

"I wanted to see—"

"You had better stop here and see it out, then," said his superior, pleasantly; "or stop, remain here till you see the signal for a fall, and then down with you like lightning; you can pull well, and you shall take an oar in my boat, do you hear?"

Harry was greatly delighted at this. He knew very well that, for his years and strength, he was reckoned a good rower, but he did not expect to be promoted to an oar in a whale boat; his uncle had told him that he must wait for this. He thanked Mr. Harris, therefore, for his kindness.

"Oh, there's no particular kindness in it," rejoined the second mate. "One of my boat's crew is on the sick list, you know, and I may as well take you as any one else; but you won't find it easy work."

Harry did not suppose it was; but that made no difference. There was one thing, however, he did not quite understand: what did Mr. Harris mean by the signal for a fall?

"You will know if you keep your ears open," he was told. "Look you, Harry: directly a fish is struck, up goes the flag-staff in the boat; and when you see this, as you will, of course, if the boats are not out of sight, what you have to do is to shout out as loud as you can, 'a fall!'—you understand?"

"Yes, sir; but if they should not be in sight?"

"They will be in sight of the captain's glass, anyhow, unless a fog rises," said Mr. Harris; "and he will sing out, whether you do or not."

"And then I am to slip down to your boat, sir?"

"Ay, ay, as quick as thought."

"And then, sir?"

"Why then you will see what is to come next," replied the second mate, as he descended leisurely.

Harry had something to do now; and in spite of the cold, which made him shiver not a little, he kept a good look out.

While the conversation had been going on, the boats had separated, and were pulling at a sharp angle with each other. The reason of this, Harry knew, was the uncertainty as to the spot where the whale would reappear. He had understood that whales did not often remain more than fifteen or twenty minutes under the water without rising to breathe; but that in that time they often swam to a great distance and with prodigious swiftness, especially if alarmed. Sometimes, he had been told, it is possible to trace the course they have taken, by an eddy, or track, on the surface of the water; but generally the pursuers are obliged to guess at this. It seemed to be so in this instance; and indeed the whale remained so long unseen, that Harry began to think that it must have escaped altogether.

But it had not escaped. It rose between the two boats, though at some distance a-head; and once more the chase was renewed. By this time, however, Harry imagined that the poor creature was in some measure aware of its danger; for, before either of the boats could reach it, it had again disappeared, and so altered its apparent course, that the pursuers were thrown out of their reckoning, and had to put about, so that the boats were once more in a straight line, that of the chief mate being considerably in advance of the other.

This time the whale rose more quickly than before, and remained longer on the surface to breathe; and again Harry saw the jets of steam spurting above its head; but before the first boat could reach within harpooning distance, there was another splash, and again the large creature was out of sight.

By this time the boats were at such a distance from the Adventurer, that Harry could only imperfectly distinguish them; indeed, they were often quite hidden from his view by the waves. Meanwhile, the ship's crew were eagerly discussing the probability of a capture, or the possibility of an escape. At length the young sailor

became aware of a sudden bustle in the
distant boats, and then he could just discern
a flag floating above one of them, accompanied by a great increase of its speed. This
was the signal, then, for which Harry was
watching; but before *he* could utter the
words, they were shouted from the crow's
nest, and caught up and repeated by all
around and below; and then there was such
a jumping and stamping on the deck, that
Harry was startled by the extraordinary
noise. He did not wait till it was over,
for he saw the crews of the different boats
rushing to lower them into the sea, and
almost tumbling over each other into them.
To slide down one of the stays, or ropes,
was the action of a few seconds; before two
minutes were expired, Harry was in Mr.
Harris' boat, with an oar in his hands; and
in another minute, that and two other boats
were gliding over the waves.

They were not wanted, however, to assist
in the capture of the whale, for that was
accomplished before they arrived at the
spot. It was Mr. Allen's harpoon which
had first struck the huge fish; and after

drawing out almost all the lines of the two
boats, and rising from time to time to
breathe, every time weaker with the vain
struggle to escape from its persecutors, the
whale had been despatched with lances, and
was floating on its back, lifeless.

Harry was astonished at the prodigious
size of the whale. As nearly as he could
measure with his eye, it was more than
fifty feet in length, and one third of this
seemed to be head. As it lay on the water
it looked like a little island; and two men
were upon it, securing it to one of the boats
by a rope which was passed through a hole
made in one of its enormous fins. This was
soon accomplished, and the men sprang back
into their boat; then all the five boats were
fastened together in a line by strong ropes,
and the boats' crews began pulling slowly
towards the ship, which was more than
two miles off, and now lying becalmed on
the water.

It was laborious work. Harry quickly
found this out, and was soon bathed in per-
spiration, although the air was piercingly
cold. But it was cheerfully performed, for

the men were in good spirits with their success, and the air rang with their joyous shouts. So laborious was the operation that two hours were consumed by it before the large whale was hauled alongside of the ship, and made fast there.

And now began another busy scene, in which the greater part of the Adventurer's crew took part. While some of the men descended on to the whale, armed with knives and "blubber spades," and other instruments, for removing the blubber; others were engaged in pumping the water out of a number of the barrels in the hold, to receive it; and others were drawing it up to the deck in large pieces weighing several hundreds of pounds each, and dividing it into smaller portions for the convenience of stowing it away. In this manner they proceeded till all the blubber was removed; then the whalebone was detached from the enormous jaws of the animal.

While all this was going on, Harry was in a boat by the side of the dead whale, in attendance on his uncle, who was superin-

tending the "flenshing," as the stripping off
the blubber is called; and after the removal
of the whalebone from the animal's mouth,
he had the curiosity to examine it closely.
It was a large mouth: the young sailor had
never imagined or even dreamed of such a
mouth as belonging to any living creature.
The great jaws being opened wide, and the
great tongue removed, the cavity was like a
large vaulted room. A ship's boat, full of
men, might have rowed into it and backed
out of it again with ease.

The work of flenshing took up some time,
but it was finished at last; and when all
the blubber and whalebone and the jaws of
the whale were removed and taken on to
the deck, the skeleton was let loose and
allowed to float away. Not unaccompanied,
however; for flocks of sea birds had been
hovering round the carcass from the time of
its capture, and some of them had been so
bold as to pounce down upon it, and fly
away with fragments of the flesh and fat,
even while the men were at work. But no
sooner was it disengaged from the ship than
the birds settled upon it, and began to

gorge themselves very greedily with the remaining blubber and flesh, which they tore from the bones. But this feast did not last long : after a little while the mutilated carcass, or "kreng," as Harry heard it called, gradually sank by its own weight, and the disturbed feeders rose in the air with loud, wild cries of disappointed hunger.

This was Harry Clark's first experience in whaling. Several more whales were caught before the season was over, and some of them gave the captors more trouble than this had done. Some also that were pursued escaped altogether from being caught, much to the disappointment of the Adventurer's crew. On one of these occasions an accident happened which will be related in its proper place. But as the young reader has perhaps had enough of whale hunting and killing in this chapter, we shall, in the next, turn to another subject.

CHAPTER VII.

SEALS AND BEARS. A DANGEROUS
ADVENTURE.

WHALES were not the only kind of living creatures with the sight of which Harry became familiar in these polar seas. One day, soon after the capture of the first whale, he was on duty on deck, when he heard one of the sailors call out, "There's a seals' wedding;" and on looking towards the quarter to which the men pointed, he perceived the surface of the sea to be thickly dotted with dark specks, which presently approached so near to the ship that he could plainly distinguish their form and features. It was a large shoal of seals; and Harry was highly amused when another sailor, who went by the name of Tom the Piper, pulled out his little flute and began to play a lively tune, which caused the seals to draw nearer still to the ship, and to pause in their course, while they stretched their

necks out of the water as far as they could
stretch them, listening to the musical sounds.

"Are they really fond of music?" Harry
asked one of the watch who was standing by.

"Seems so: they always do stop and
listen when music is played to them. I
have seen it scores of times; and they will
cock up their heads if there is only a
whistle."

It was very interesting to watch these
harmless creatures. They were evidently
very timid; and while they were attracted
to the side of the ship by Tom the Piper's
sweet sounds, they were so watchful that
every movement gave them alarm, and
caused them to dive under water. They
were as quick of sight, too, as of hearing;
for when a gun was fired at one of the
shoal which had ventured nearer than the
rest to the ship, the flash warned the poor
animal of its danger, and before the bullet
could reach it, it had dived, and presently
came up again unhurt.

Harry was glad of this. He thought
it was treacherous to entice the seals in

that way to their destruction. "Don't you think so, uncle?" he asked.

"That depends on circumstances, Harry," replied Mr. Allen, playfully. "Suppose we wanted seal very much, and seal would not come near without being enticed; what then?"

"But we don't want seal very much, do we, uncle?" retorted Harry.

"No, I cannot say that we do; but that does not answer my question exactly."

"Well, I suppose if we did," said Harry, musing a little—"I suppose—but, uncle, what could we ever want seals for?" he asked.

"For more purposes than one," rejoined his uncle. "So much so that some ships are fitted out almost entirely for the seal fishery. And sometimes whale ships which have failed in taking whales have partly made up for the disappointment and loss by catching seals."

"But what are they good for?" Harry still wished to know.

"They yield a very excellent oil," he was told; "especially in the spring of the

year, when they are very fat. At this time
a large seal will produce several gallons
of oil; besides this, the skins make good
leather, and the flesh is not unpleasant food."

After this, Harry had an opportunity of
observing one of these creatures more
closely. It was at a time when the Adventurer was beset with ice, and so becalmed
as well that the crew had little to engage
their attention besides constant and careful
watchfulness for the safety of the ship.
Many excursions on the ice were made at
this time, in which Harry was sometimes
permitted to join, as a relief from the
monotony of ship board. On one of these
expeditions, the rovers came upon a number
of seals near a rift in the ice, towards which
the timid animals speedily scuttled away.
But in their flight, one of their number—a
very young and little one—was left behind;
and Harry, running before it, intercepted
its flight and secured it.

The baby-seal began then to cry pite-
ously, in a tone very much resembling
that of a child, as well as to struggle to
get away from its captor. Harry, however,

held it tight, and returned with it in triumph to the ship. He was good-naturedly laughed at by his shipmates and officers for his strange fancy, but the little foundling was taken on deck, and very soon became the pet of the whole crew.

At first, the young seal was very shy, and refused to eat what was offered it. But after a day or two it became more reconciled to its confinement, and readily took food from Harry's hand. Before long, it began to roam, in its awkward way, about the deck, and to thrust its broad flat nose against the sailors, as though soliciting their attention. Harry had some thought of taking the curious animal back with him to England, and making a present of it to the Zoological Garden in London; but one day, when the gangway was open, the captive scuttled towards it, and before any one could stay its progress, had slipped over the ship's side and plunged into the sea.

I am not sure that Harry was very sorry for this loss. He had become fond of his pet, certainly; but he knew that it was not in its natural element and state of freedom; and that, however kindly treated, it would be much happier when at liberty. Besides, he found it difficult to provide it with its natural and proper food at all times; and long before the voyage was over, Harry had quite enough to do without having the care of a tamed seal.*

* Seals are very easily tamed; and if they are taken young, and well used, they soon learn to know their keepers, and evince nearly the same attachment to them as dogs do. Of course, in order to be properly in their element, they must have access to the water, which is essential to their comfort, though not to their mere existence.

A seal which was captured young was kept for a considerable time by some soldiers on one of the small islets in the Frith of Forth, and it showed so strong an attachment to them that though it often went into the water it never showed any disposition to escape. If they threw a piece of stick into the sea, the seal was instantly after it, in the same way as a water spaniel; and all its amusing tricks very much resembled those of the more playful varieties of dogs.

It slept in the little barrack which had been erected for the men, and during the day it was very fond of getting into their beds. Its entrance into them was effected with tolerable expedition; but to descend was a more difficult matter, as it was apt to tumble: and at last it was killed by one of these falls.

While the Adventurer was surrounded
with ice, several polar bears made their
appearance; and on one occasion, Harry
had a narrow escape from one of them.
He was on the ice with Mr. Harris, the
second mate, at some distance from the
ship. Mr. Harris had a gun; and Harry,
without any particular purpose, was armed
with a whale lance.

"Halt! Harry," exclaimed Mr. Harris,
in a low whisper, and holding back his
young companion: "what do you see
yonder?" and he pointed with his gun to
a distant part of the ice which was crowded
with hummocks.

"There's something moving, sir," said
Harry; and the next moment he added,
"It is a bear, Mr. Harris."

"Ay, ay: keep quiet, and we will see
if we cannot secure a bear's skin. The
animal does not see us yet, I think:" and
Mr. Harris began to creep very cautiously
towards the hummocks, followed by his
young companion, who no doubt fancied
it would be a feather in both their caps if
they could kill a bear and take back its skin.

Meanwhile the bear continued to move about the ice hills unconscious of its adversaries, until they had reached within what Mr. Harris called fair shooting distance; and then concealing himself behind a hummock, and motioning to Harry to do the same, he carefully examined his gun, loaded it with another bullet, and then, creeping still nearer to the huge beast, he raised it to his shoulder and fired.

The next moment, a loud ferocious growl warned the sportsmen that, if wounded, their anticipated prey was not killed; and before Mr. Harris could reload his gun, the enraged animal rushed towards his enemies with open mouth and glaring eyes.

"Your lance!" shouted Mr. Harris, throwing down his gun; and, snatching the lance out of Harry's hand, he stood for a moment on the defensive. It was but for a moment; for the bear was already close to them, and twisting the weapon out of the mate's hand, he seized it in his mouth, and snapped asunder the iron shaft as though it had been only a rotten stick.

"We must run for it now, Harry," cried

Mr. Harris; and they both started off at full speed without stopping to recover the gun or broken lance.

It was well for them both that the bear was wounded in its shoulder, which made it slower in its movements than it would otherwise have been; and, also, that it halted for a few seconds to sniff at and walk round the abandoned gun: thus the disarmed and defenceless hunters were enabled to gain a few yards in advance of their infuriated foe. But they were not able long to retain this slight advantage: after a few minutes, the heavy breathing of the bear was heard behind them; and, on looking over his shoulder, Harry perceived, with dismay, that the savage beast was almost close at their heels.

It was a race for life; but the presence of mind of the two sailors did not forsake them. Harry remembered being told by his uncle of a man who, in similar circumstances, escaped from a bear by throwing down first one then another of his garments; and he tried the experiment of dropping his cap. This so far succeeded that

ESCAPE FROM THE BEAR.

the bear stopped for some seconds in his pursuit to smell the cap, and to tear it into shreds in wrath. This enabled Harry and his companion to gain a few yards upon their pursuer. Mr. Harris's cap went next, and then his pea-jacket; then Harry's pea-jacket, which all shared the same fate as the first cap, and with the same result of delaying the savage animal in the pursuit; so that the rash man and boy approached nearer to their place of refuge than they had at first dared to hope.

All their efforts, however, would have proved unavailing—and, indeed, Harry had given himself up for lost, and already fancied that he felt the hot breath of the bear scorching his cheeks—if help had not arrived from the ship. Happily, the attention or curiosity of one of the sailors on board had been drawn to the fearful chase; and as soon as the alarm was given, a strong party of the crew hastened to the rescue of their distressed and despairing shipmates. When the bear saw how matters stood, he first halted, and then, probably alarmed by the shouts of the sailors, turned with a growl of

disappointment, and endeavoured to escape.
Then came another part of the adventure.
While the two rescued ones sat down on
the ice to recover breath, their companions
started off in chase of the bear; and after
a sharp but short hunt they succeeded in
overtaking it. The poor animal had but
little chance after this; for whichever way
it turned, sharp lances were levelled against
it; and very soon its dead carcass was
hauled to the ship's side in triumph.

It was a large creature, and looked formidable even when dead; for it was seven
or eight feet in length, and large in pro-
portion. Its huge limbs and strong horny
claws gave an idea of prodigious power,
and the strength of its jaws and sharp teeth
had been shown in the ease with which it
had snapped in two the iron lance.

The second mate and Harry did not ob-
tain much renown by their misadventure;
and indeed, they were both rather sharply
rebuked by the captain, for putting themselves unnecessarily into peril, and for their
fool-hardiness in attacking so dangerous an
animal when at so great a distance from

the ship. This did not prevent them, however, from eating a hearty meal of bear steaks, which Harry thought almost as good as beef; and the skin, which afterwards fell to his lot, when dressed, provided him with a warm coverlet, which kept him warm through many a sharp frosty night.

The Adventurer was not long beset with ice, which, after a few days, began to break up into large masses, and to float gradually away with the current, while the ship's crew, taking advantage of a fair wind, once more worked their vessel on to the open sea. And though they never passed many days without seeing ice near them, either in the form of drift, floe, berg, or field, as the summer advanced, it became more fragile and shifting. Meanwhile, the sailors were kept in a state of constant excitement and watchfulness, day and night, by the great object of the voyage.

CHAPTER VIII.

THE DANGER OF EVIL COMMUNICATIONS. A FATAL
ACCIDENT.

EVERAL whales were caught and dealt with in the manner already described; but I shall pass over these events, merely saying that Harry Clark, although young, proved himself so efficient in a whale-boat that he was often permitted to accompany his uncle, as one of the rowers. But there was a whale hunt which I must notice, as showing one of the numerous dangers to which sailors in whaling ships are exposed.

There was the usual look out from the crow's nest. It was night, but a night almost as light as day, for the summer sun in those high latitudes does not sink below the horizon, even at midnight, for many weeks in succession; but shows its broad red face, like a large full moon. And now it was near midsummer.

It was a kind of day-night therefore, and objects could be discerned from the crow's nest of the Adventurer for many miles round. There were ice-floes rather near to the ship, but the ice was rotten and unsafe to venture on; and there were icebergs further off, towering up towards the sky, with their sharp pinnacles in many fantastic varieties, glittering in the pale sunshine, and sometimes sending out sparkles of light like diamonds. Other whaling ships were visible around; for it was full season now, and the Arctic Ocean was busy and gay with these summer visitors.

A long distance off might be seen the mountains of Spitzbergen; for though whalers seldom touch upon that inhospitable coast, their fishing ground extends to it, and it is often in sight.

The night was very quiet and still. There was not much wind; and the topsails, which were set to catch any little breath of it, flapped idly against the masts. This was almost the only sound that was heard, save the quiet footsteps of the watch on deck, as they paced to and fro, wrapped

H

in their pea-jackets, worsted mittens, and fur caps: for they needed these helps to comfort, though it was summer.

Harry was leaning over the bulwarks in a thoughtful mood. It was not his watch; but he could not sleep, and he had gone on deck to look around him. Presently a hand was laid upon his shoulder, and on turning round, he faced the second mate.

Harry was a favourite with Mr. Harris, for whom he had a strong feeling of regard in turn. It was this that had led them into companionship in the adventure with the bear; and Harry was gratified at being noticed and encouraged by one whom he felt to be so much his superior, and on whom he had no claim for friendship.

Harry's uncle had witnessed this intimacy with some concern. He knew that Mr. Harris was not a safe companion for an inexperienced youth; and he had quietly endeavoured to put Harry on his guard. Harry himself did not see so clearly where the danger was, and in what it consisted.

And yet if Harry had examined himself very closely he might have discovered before

now that some of his relish for religion was
gone ; that he did not consult his Christian
chart so steadily and so frequently as at the
beginning of the voyage ; that thoughts
sometimes came into his mind which had no
business there; and that he did not pray so
earnestly as he should have done to be
delivered from temptation, and kept from
standing in the way of sinners, and from
walking in the way of the ungodly.

Yes, Harry was in danger : that is to say,
his soul was in danger, though he did not
know it; and it was in the greater danger
because of this.

Some of Harry's danger arose from his
neglect of watchfulness. All Christians are
enjoined to "watch and pray," lest they
enter into temptation ; and it is not reason-
able to suppose that such a youth as our
young sailor could stand fast in the ways of
true piety, while disregarding this injunc-
tion. But this danger was increased by the
influence of an ungodly companion. He
might have known this if he had thought
about it.

Mr. Harris and Harry leaned over the

bulwarks together, and soon entered into
conversation. It is not necessary to set
down the whole of this conversation. It
was begun by Mr. Harris, who spoke, first
of all, about the scenery around them:
then he talked of other scenes he had
witnessed in former voyages, and of his
past adventures. This led him to tell of
some of his old shipmates, and especially
of one who was nicknamed "Bible Bill,"
because of his fondness for reading the
Bible. Mr. Harris spoke very ill-naturedly
of this man, and in a tone of contempt both
for him and his practice. From this, the
conversation went on to more serious
matters; and Mr. Harris spoke out more
plainly than Harry had ever before heard
him speak about the Scriptures, which he
mentioned in such terms as I must not
repeat, and which shocked Harry to hear;
and also about those who profess to believe
them. At length, Harry mustered courage
to say—

"Mr. Harris, I wish you would not talk
such things to me."

"Why not? You cannot say that they

are not true. Don't you know that it is all
a sham and a cheat? Come now, Harry,
tell me what you really think, and no
nonsense."

· "I don't think that what you say is true,
Mr. Harris," said Harry, modestly, though
earnestly, for his feelings were roused: "I
am sure it cannot be, though you think so,
of course. And I am sure it is not all a
cheat. There is uncle Gilbert, now; you
cannot think that he is a cheat; and Captain
Smith, again; and others on board who
believe the Bible and are Christians: you
do not mean to say that they are all
cheats?"

"Oh, I have nothing to say against the
captain, nor against Mr. Allen, either,"
replied the second mate, lightly laughing;
"so you need not colour up, Harry. They
are plain-sailing enough, though it might
be possible to take a reef or two out of
their sails, perhaps, if it were to come to
fending and proving. But if we must not
call them cheats, we may say they are
cheated, eh?"

No, Harry would not allow that, either.

Why should they be cheated? he wanted to know.

"Because

> 'the pleasure is as great
> In being cheated, as to cheat.'"

said Mr. Harris, laughing again.

"Then perhaps it is you who are being cheated, sir," retorted Harry; "only you may not know it."

The conversation had got as far as this when it was suddenly put a stop to by a loud shout from the crow's nest, that a number of whales were in sight, some distance from the Adventurer. It did not take much time to rouse the sleepers below; and in a very few minutes all the boats were let down and started off in pursuit, leaving only the master and seven or eight hands on board to work the ship. This time Harry was in the boat which had Mr. Harris for harpooner.

It was not long before the boats got near the whales. There were four or five very close together; and so skilful and cautious had the boats' crews been in their movements, that three whales were harpooned almost at the same time.

It is not my intention to describe another whale chase, and I shall leave to be imagined the sudden diving of the stricken fish, the rapid running out of the lines, the swift cutting of the boat through the water, which rose almost to their gunwales, the bailing out of the water from the boats, the violent exertions of the rowers, and the excitement of all concerned.

Five hours passed away, and in this time two of the whales had been killed; and the crews of the five boats which had succeeded in their capture rowed away to the assistance of their companions, whom they could distinguish at a long distance off, still engaged in the pursuit of the one remaining.

They got nearer and nearer, and could see the exhausted fish rising for the last time to the surface, and could also see the jets of steam and red-coloured water, thrown up from its blow holes, which showed that it would soon be dead. Then they heard the hearty shouts of their companions, and rowed still harder, that they might be ready to give any help that was needed.

For a minute or two the whale lay quiet on the surface of the water; and then it began slowly to turn over on its back, as whales always do when dead or dying; and the successful whalers eagerly rowed up to it to gather in the lines and to secure it for towing towards the ship. At this moment the voice of Mr. Harris, whose harpoon had first struck the whale, and whose boat was nearest to it, was heard to shout—

"Back water, men! back water for your lives!"

The warning came too late; already the dying fish had collected its last remaining strength: it could no longer dive; but, in its death flurry, as the whalers call it, it raised its enormous tail; and in another moment the boat was destroyed by a single blow, and all its crew were plunged into the deep water.

This was not the worst that had happened. There had been six men in the boat besides Harry; but when the other boats came up to the rescue of the struggling swimmers, only four could be seen. Harry was one of these, and he was picked up unhurt; so were two other of the rowers. Mr. Harris also was floating on the surface of the water; but when he was taken into one of the boats, it was found that he was senseless: he had been so crushed with the blow that very little life seemed to remain in him. He only just breathed. There were three men yet missing; but there were no signs of them on the water For a long time two of the boats rowed round and round the whale, which was now quite dead, and among the fragments of the broken boat which were floating about; but at last they had to give up the search. The poor whalers had sunk beneath the waves.

Meanwhile, the unhappy second mate was conveyed, as swiftly as oars could be pulled, to the ship. He was taken on board and carried to his berth, where the captain himself employed all the means in his power to restore him to consciousness, and, if possible, to life.

There were no more hearty, joyous shouts

that day. The whales were towed to the
ship, of course, and the usual work of
flenshing went on busily as ever; but the
men were silent and thoughtful: they were
thinking of their poor drowned shipmates,
and the dying man, so near to them.

CHAPTER IX.

A DEATH-BED SCENE.

EVERAL days passed away. The weather was wild and stormy; but not so wild and stormy as the thoughts of the dying man, as he lay, crushed and helpless and moaning, in his berth below.

All that skill and kindness could attempt for the relief of his sufferings had been attempted; but there was no hope that Mr. Harris could survive many days; it was more likely that a few hours would terminate his mortal life.

Gilbert Allen was by his side in the little cabin. He had been praying for his poor suffering fellow-officer, and an open Bible was in his hand. He had been reading such encouraging passages as these:—

"As I live, saith the Lord, I have no pleasure in the death of the wicked; but that the wicked turn from his way and

live."* "Come now, and let us reason together, saith the Lord : though your sins be
as scarlet, they shall be as white as snow;
though they be red like crimson, they shall
be as wool."† "Seek ye the Lord while he
may be found, call ye upon him while he is
near. Let the wicked forsake his way, and
the unrighteous man his thoughts; and let
him return unto the Lord, and he will have
mercy upon him; and to our God, for he
will abundantly pardon. For my thoughts
are not your thoughts, neither are your
ways my ways, saith the Lord. For as the
heavens are high above the earth, so are
my ways higher than your ways, and my
thoughts than your thoughts." ‡

Then, having repeated these words from
the Old Testament, the pious mate turned
to the New, and with much emotion read
other passages :—

"This is a faithful saying, and worthy of
all acceptation, that Christ Jesus came into
the world to save sinners." § "God com-
mendeth his love towards us, in that, while

---

* Ezekiel xxxiii. 11.   † Isaiah i. 18.   ‡ Isaiah lv. 6—9.
§ 1 Timothy i. 15.

we were yet sinners, Christ died for us." *
" God so loved the world, that he gave
his only begotten Son, that whosoever be-
lieveth in him should not perish, but have
everlasting life."† " If we say that we have
no sin, we deceive ourselves, and the truth
is not in us. If we confess our sins, He is
faithful and just to forgive us our sins, and
to cleanse us from all unrighteousness." ‡
" For Christ also hath once suffered, the
just for the unjust, that he might bring
us to God." § " Him hath God exalted
with his right hand to be a Prince and a
Saviour, to give repentance . . . and for-
giveness of sins." ‖ " Wherefore he is able
also to save them to the uttermost that come
unto God by him, seeing he ever liveth to
make intercession for them." ¶

The dying man heard these words, and
once or twice his lips moved as though he
would have spoken ; but no sound came
from them, until the Christian mate had
closed the book : then the unhappy man
said faintly, though without difficulty, for

* Romans v. 8.   † John iii. 16.   ‡ 1 John i. 8, 9.
§ 1 Peter iii. 18.   ‖ Acts v. 31.   ¶ Hebrews vii. 25.

crushed and mortally injured as he was, speaking was not painful to him—

"I expect I know what you are going to say, Mr. Allen; but it is of no use."

"I cannot leave you so, my poor friend," said Gilbert Allen, soothingly. "Think of your present condition."

"I know that well enough; I know that I am going, if that is what you mean."

"It is very true; it would be cruel in me to try to give you hope of recovery: there is none."

This was quite certain, there was no hope. The poor man's limbs had begun to mortify, and death had already commenced its work. Gilbert Allen knew this, and it made him very sorrowful.

"No, I know there is no hope," said Mr. Harris.

"But there is a hope set before us in the gospel, of eternal life, if we do but flee for refuge to lay hold upon it," said Mr. Allen, earnestly, and with tears rolling down his manly cheeks. "Think of this, my poor friend. Think of Him who came to save us from the pains and miseries of the second death. Think of that precious word I have just read to you, that Jesus Christ came into the world to save sinners, and that he is able to save to the uttermost them that come to God by him."

He waited for an answer; but none came. Then he spoke again, more tenderly than before, if that were possible.

"Think of the blessed Saviour, Harris, who never cast out any that come to God by him. God says to you now, in his word, 'Believe on the Lord Jesus Christ, and thou shalt be saved.' Think how he saved the poor thief on the cross, in his last agonies. Pray to him, pray to him now, to save you; and if you pray from your heart, he'll do it, the Almighty Saviour will. Say to him, as was said to him once at sea, 'Lord, save; or I perish;'—as the blind man said to him, 'Jesus, thou Son of David, have mercy on me!' Give yourself up to him to bless you with his forgiving love and mercy; and he will do it. He can take away your sins, my poor friend, and wash your soul in his own blood, and fit it to go from this poor broken-down prison, to his heavenly kingdom. Don't you know this? don't you believe it? Pray to him now—now—before it is too late: 'Seek the Lord while he may be found; call upon him while he is near.'"

Oh, how earnest was the Christian sailor! How tenderly, and yet how faithfully, he reminded his dying shipmate that in a few hours he would be beyond the reach of mercy; that his soul was sinking, sinking, sinking into eternal death; but that yet there was a gracious hand held out to save him, if he would be saved.

"Oh, if I could think so!" said the dying man, very sadly: "but you don't know what I have been, Mr. Allen. But there's one thing I can do; and I'll do it," he said, with a good deal of energy. "Allen, I want to see your nephew, Harry Clark—and I must see him alone: will you send him down to me? Do. I don't mean him any harm, I promise you that: I fear I have done him some already. Send him down to me, please; and at once. It is the last thing I shall ask of you, I expect." He said this very imploringly.

"I'll send him to you, Harris," said Harry's uncle; and presently Harry was by the dying man's berth.

"Harry, you remember what I said to you the other night; and what you said to me?"

Yes, Harry remembered.

"I told you that I did not believe the Bible, and that religion was all a cheat, you know."

"Yes, you did, sir," said Harry, in a troubled voice.

"And you said that perhaps I was being cheated, did you not?"

"I hope you do not mind my having said so, Mr. Harris," replied our sailor boy.

"Mind! Oh no: I did not mind it then, and I don't mind it now. I want to tell you something, Harry," the poor man went on, in a hollow, mournful tone; "I want to tell you that you were right, and I was wrong; and that you are not to mind anything I have ever said to you about the Bible. The Bible is true; and I have been cheated, as you said. You don't

I

know who it is that has cheated me : I'll
tell you—I have cheated myself. Don't
you cheat yourself, Harry."

Harry was so overcome that he could
not reply.

"I was brought up to read the Bible.
My father was a good man; he was a
Christian ; and when I was a boy, like
you, I fancied I should be a Christian some
day or other, in regular order. When I
first went to sea I had a Bible in my chest,
and meant to read it. But I got laughed
at, Harry, and then I was ashamed to be
seen with it in my hands. Then after that I
never was seen with it in my hands. Then
I—but I need not tell you any more about
myself; that is not why I sent for you."

He was silent for a minute or two: his
mind seemed to wander, and his countenance changed, so that Harry fancied that
he would never speak again. But presently
the dying man revived a little, and went on.

"What was I saying? Oh, I know: I
sent for you to tell you not to be turned
away from thinking about religion by such
fools as I am. The Bible is REAL, Harry ;

and religion is a real thing and not a sham;
and Jesus Christ is— " He stopped short
here, as though some thoughts came into
his mind too painful to be uttered; at least,
Harry thought so.

"The Lord Jesus Christ is a great,
almighty Saviour, Mr. Harris," whispered
Harry, while tears sprang from his eyes.

The poor man shook his head mournfully.
"He will soon be my Judge," he said.

Harry was very sorrowful. He knew
that what the dying man said was true:
but he thought also of the gracious promises of God to *all* who turn penitently
and believingly to him.

"Won't you let me read to you out of the
Bible, Mr. Harris?" he pleaded; and as
Mr. Harris did not forbid his doing so, he
took the book which his uncle had left
behind, and opened it. Harry did not
know what part it would be best to read
from; but he knew he could not do wrong
in reading about the sufferings of the Lord
Jesus Christ as he hung on the cross, as a
sacrifice for sin, and about the penitent
malefactor to whom the dying Saviour

spoke such pardoning, loving words, in the last hour of that great sinner's life.

"Thank you, Harry," said the mate, when Harry had done reading. "It is very kind of you; and I'll — yes, you have given me something to think about, Harry."

"And you will pray—pray for pardon and mercy, Mr. Harris — pray for God's Holy Spirit to help—to help you to believe?" Harry sobbed.

"I'll try, Harry: yes, I think I'll try."

"I think I must go now, sir," said Harry.

"Yes, go; you have done me good— a little good, I think, Harry. Perhaps I shall see you again, before—; but if I shouldn't—" He held out his hand, and pressed it and said, "Good bye." Then Harry slowly withdrew from the cabin.

Harry never saw Mr. Harris again, in life. After lingering a few hours longer, the poor man died. It never was known— it never can be known on earth—whether his last few hours were employed in seeking mercy through the Redeemer. Harry

hoped that they were; and that He whose
promises are so full and free, gave, even at
last, the Holy Spirit, to sanctify and prepare the soul of the dying man for the
solemn change from life to death. But he
could only hope this.

That night there was a funeral at sea.
Harry stood by when the body of the
second mate, sewed up in a hammock, was
committed to the deep; and he heard the
solemn words of the funeral service, but
they fell upon his ears with a sorrowful
sound. He remembered another funeral
at sea which he had witnessed, and another
death-bed at sea by which he had stood;*
and he thought of the contrast between the
closing scenes of a Christian's life, and those
of one who had so long despised the Lord
Jesus Christ. And when he was by himself, he prayed very fervently and earnestly
for pardon for past remissness, and for the
indwelling of God's good Spirit to lead
and keep him in the narrow path that leads
to life everlasting.

* See "HARRY THE SAILOR BOY," page 110.

CHAPTER X.

THE Adventurer's voyage was drawing to a close. The fishing had been successful. Nearly three hundred tons of blubber and whalebone were stowed away in the hold, and the crew were rejoicing in the expectation of setting sail southward.

The short summer of the north was rapidly passing away. Every day the sun dipped deeper and deeper below the horizon, and was longer in making its re-appearance. In a few weeks, the long winter night would set in. The sea, which for a time had been open, and in some measure free from ice, began to close in; and the ice itself became every day firmer. Packs of drift ice formed themselves into floes; and floes began to cement together into fields. At last the welcome word was given; and with hearty goodwill all the crew made preparations for the return home.

The health of the crew was good; and, excepting the sad occurrence which I have recorded, life and limb had been preserved.

Harry was saying something like this to his uncle one day, when the sails were all set, and the Adventurer was ploughing its way through a smooth sea.

" Ay, ay, we have cause to be thankful; but we must not boast, Harry, as if our skill had done it; and we may have a check yet," said the more experienced seaman.

A few hours afterwards a heavy fog arose, the first they had experienced for many weeks, and this was accompanied by a sharp freezing wind from the north, which made the hardiest sailors shiver and shrink, while Harry was reminded of a passage in one of the Psalms: " He sendeth forth his commandment upon earth; his word runneth very swiftly. He giveth snow like wool; he scattereth the hoar frost like ashes. He casteth forth his ice like morsels: who can stand before his cold ? " *

* Psalm cxlvii. 15—17.

It was wonderful how rapidly the appearance of all things became changed. The sea altered in its colour, and looming through the fog could be dimly discerned large masses of ice tumbling onwards, and fraught with destruction to any craft that stood in their way. You may be sure that a good look out was now kept from the crow's nest; and by God's providence the Adventurer escaped injury.

Then the wind suddenly shifted, blowing strongly from the south-west; and there was danger that the ship would be driven violently against the ice among which it was now entangled.

For several hours the Adventurer was thus driven, but happily without accident; when an order was shouted from the crow's nest to put the helm hard-a-lee.

" Ay, ay, sir ; hard-a-lee it is," shouted in reply the man at the helm; and in a few minutes the course of the ship was so far altered as to show the startled sailors the imminent peril to which they had unconsciously been exposed. An enormous iceberg, previously hidden by the thick fog,

"BLESS THE LORD FOR THIS DELIVERANCE!"

was right a-head; and had the order been
given a minute later, or been less promptly
obeyed, the ship would have struck and
been an instant wreck. As it was, the
Adventurer almost touched it in drifting
past; and horror was depicted on more
than one countenance as the sailors manned
the yards and stood to the helm.

"Bless the Lord for this deliverance!"
exclaimed the first mate devoutly.

In another moment a curious alteration
had taken place. The fog was so far dis-
persed that the iceberg could be seen lifting
up its high massive peaks a hundred feet
or more above the topmasts of the ship,
and apparently motionless in the sea, while
all around the smaller pieces of ice were
being carried by the wind and current
swiftly northward. The Adventurer was
in the lee of the berg, and sheltered by
it from the storm.

There was a rapid consultation between
the captain and his mate; and then boats
were lowered; an anchor and cable were
conveyed to the iceberg, and made fast;
and then, while the loose ice floated past,

the ship remained in comparatively smooth water, being sheltered by that which had so nearly proved its destruction.

For many hours, the ship was thus securely moored to the iceberg, until the wind abated and became more favourable; then the sailors gladly obeyed the order to take in the anchor, and set sail. They were not sorry to remove from the vicinity of the sheltering ice mountain, grand as it was to look upon; and they were pleased to know that, wind permitting, there was nothing to detain them longer in those polar regions.

It was happy for them that they had thus promptly obeyed their captain's order. The Adventurer was scarcely more than a mile from the iceberg; and Harry, standing by the side of his uncle, was admiring the brilliant appearance it presented, when a sudden movement was observed in the entire mass; it seemed to be split in sunder, and, after a momentary suspense, a large portion of it was detached from the solid mountain, toppled over, and fell with a hideous crash into the foaming water beneath. Then came a huge swelling wave, on and on, until it reached the ship, which it lifted high upon its crest, as though she had been but a cork; then leaving her in the trough beneath, it hastened onward in its course, while the agitated sea around became white with foam.

The voice of praise rose that day from many a heart and lip on board the Adventurer; and Harry heartily joined in the public thanksgiving offered by the pious captain for the mercy experienced in this great deliverance.

*　　*　　*　　*　　*

From this time all was smooth sailing. Every day's sail carried the Adventurer nearer home. Before winter set in in England, the good ship had safely arrived at port; and the crew having been paid off, Harry once more set his face towards Hazel-hurst, accompanied by his uncle.

It had been a profitable voyage to Harry, as well as to his superiors and shipmates: and he was glad to believe that his well-filled purse would be useful to his widowed mother. He had a good many histories

to tell, too, of his adventures and escapes.
All this was pleasant; but there was one
recollection which weighed heavily on his
mind. He thought of the poor second mate,
and of the sudden death of his companions
in the whaling boat. But while he thought
of these, with subdued feelings of sorrow,
he felt grateful that the solemn lessons
there brought to him had not, as he hoped
and believed, been wasted on his soul,
and that he could adopt as his own the
words of a hymn that he remembered :—

    " Amazing grace that kept my breath,
      Nor bid my soul remove,
    Till I had learned my Saviour's death,
      And well insured his love."

Books for Young People

PUBLISHED BY THE

RELIGIOUS TRACT SOCIETY.

————◆————

Jessica's First Prayer. Illustrated. Royal 16mo. 1s. cloth boards; 1s. 6d. extra, gilt edges.

By the same Author, each with Engravings.

Bede's Charity. Crown 8vo. 4s. extra cloth boards, gilt edges.

Max Kromer. A Story of the Siege of Strasbourg. Royal 16mo. 1s. 6d. cloth boards; 2s. extra, gilt edges.

Fern's Hollow. Crown 8vo. 2s. cloth boards; 2s. 6d. extra, gilt edges.

Fishers of Derby Haven. Crown 8vo. 2s. cloth boards; 2s. 6d. extra, gilt edges.

Pilgrim Street. A Story of Manchester Life. Crown 8vo. 2s. cloth boards; 2s. 6d. extra, gilt edges.

Alone in London. Royal 16mo. 1s. 6d. cloth boards; 2s. extra, gilt edges.

Little Meg's Children. Royal 16mo. 1s. 1s. 6d. cloth boards; 2s. extra, gilt edges.

The Natural History Scrap-Book. With Large Engravings by the best Artists, and descriptive Letterpress. Part I.—ANIMALS. Part II.—BIRDS, FISHES, ETC. Imperial oblong 8vo. Each part 2s. in Coloured Cover. Complete in cloth, handsomely bound, gilt edges, 4s.

Golden Sayings for the Young. With fine Engravings. Imperial 8vo. 4s. cloth boards, gilt edges.

Janet Darney's Story. A Tale of Fisher Life in Chale Bay. By SARAH DOUDNEY. Crown 8vo. 3s. 6d. gilt edges.

Peter the Apprentice. A Historical Tale of the Reformation in England. Engravings. Fcap. 8vo. 2s. cloth boards; 2s. 6d. gilt edges.

City Sparrows, and Who cared for Them. By RUTH LYNN. Fcap. 8vo. 2s. cloth boards; 2s. 6d. gilt edges.

Vivian and his Friends; or, Two Hundred Years ago. By G. E. SARGENT. With Engravings. Imperial 16mo. 3s. 6d. cloth, gilt edges.

The Cheery Chime of Garth, and Other Stories. By Mrs. PROSSER, Author of "Original Fables," "Quality Fogg's Old Ledger," etc. With Illustrations. Fcap 8vo. 1s. 6d. cloth boards.

Pictures for our Pets. Profusely illustrated. Quarto. Each Part in fancy boards, 2s.; or, together, bound in cloth, gilt edges, 3s. 6d.; handsomely bound, 4s. 6d.

The Realm of the Ice King. By the Author of "Saved from the Wreck," etc. Numerous Illustrations. Imperial 16mo. 4s. 6d. cloth boards, gilt edges.

LONDON: THE RELIGIOUS TRACT SOCIETY.

CPSIA information can be obtained at www.ICGtesting.com
Printed in the USA
LVOW04s1303070515

437605LV00002B/298/P